THE T.R.U.T.H OF MARRIAGE

DESPINA G. NICOLAOU

Copyright © 2016 Despina G. Nicolaou

All rights reserved.

First Published in the **UK** by **DVG STAR** Publishing

ISBN: 0992869471
ISBN-13:978-0992869472

DEDICATION

This book is dedicated to the three men of my life.
To my husband George Georgiades, who was always next to me in good and bad times, supporting me, caring of me, loving me and above all believing in me.
It is also dedicated to my two sons Photis and Mario Georgiades.
Two great sons that always made me feel very proud of them. From the day they were born until today both of them showed to me their love and respect in different ways.
These three men supported me and encouraged me to write this book.

THANK YOU VERY MUCH FOR BEING IN MY LIFE!

NOTE TO THE READER

I would like to say that my aim is to share my knowledge and experience about marriage as a woman with other women.

Sometimes it may seem that what I propose in this book is like to be woman's obligation and that man has nothing to do.

Because I don't want such a misunderstanding to arise, I would like to make clear that for a marriage to be a successful one it needs the participation of both, the husband and wife.

Their role is equally important
"It takes two to tango". I decided not to give advice and tips for men in this book because it would be complicated and confusing. I just wanted my message for women to be clear and replete.

Also, I want to address to those women who did not manage to make their marriage happy despite all their efforts, that:

"Do not stay in a sick, negative, problematic situation. Take action as soon as you can. The sooner the better. Every woman has the right to the pleasure. You have to live to your full potential and not neglecting yourself by doing things that give joy and pleasure to others only.

But I hope my book "THE T.R.U.T.H OF MARRIAGE" will help you and become a useful tool when you meet the right man and together you will walk the path of your earthly life.

The information, including opinion and analysis, contained herein is based on the author's personal experiences and is not intended to provide professional advice.

The author and the publisher make no warranties, either expressed or implied, concerning the accuracy, applicability, effectiveness, reliability or suitability of the contents. If you wish to apply or follow the advice or recommendations mentioned herein, you take full responsibility for your actions. The author and publisher of this book shall in no event be held liable for any direct, indirect, incidental or consequential damages arising directly or indirectly from the use of any of the information contained in this book.
All content is for information only and is not warranted for content accuracy or any other implied or explicit purpose.

CONTENTS

ACKNOWLEDGMENTS i

FOREWORD v

PROLOQUE 1

TRUTH #1 *RESPECT* 5

TABLE 1 – *WITH NO RESPECT* 10

TABLE 2 – *WITH RESPECT* 11

TRUTH #2 *PATIENCE* 13

TRUTH #3 *TRUST* 21

TRUTH # 4 *PASSION* 27

TRUTH # 5 *LOVE* 35

TRUTH #6 *LOYALTY* 45

TRUTH #7 *HONESTY* 51

TRUTH #8 *ATTITUDE* 59

TRUTH # 9 *COMMUNICATION* 67

TRUTH #10 *FRIENDSHIP* 75

EPILOGUE 81

ABOUT THE AUTHOR 83

TESTIMONIALS 85

ACKNOWLEDGMENTS

I am eternally grateful to my mentor **Philip Chan**, a successful International teacher, the 10-Seconds Math's Expert, Award Winning Author and two times best seller in Amazon.
Philip as a philanthropist, giving his love, is the person that believed in me and showed to me with disinterested love the way to make my dream come true. Sincere grateful thanks for his invaluable tips, for his advice for my first book and his guidance on my new career as an author.

I am also grateful to **Marina Nani,** Author and founder of RADIO W.O.R.K.S WORLD, for all her wonderful support and encouragement. Marina is a person who also believes in values and to the beauty of marriage and family. As soon as she heard about my forthcoming book 'THE T.R.U.T.H OF MARRIAGE' she constantly encouraged me to focus on the right things. I'd like to thank her for her inspirational
teaching and for giving me the chance to become the "Family Matters Host" of RADIO W.O.R.K.S WORLD and sharing with her this incredible journey.

I'd like to mention **J.T Foxx, Gerry Roberts** and **Andy Harrington.**
All super coaches and number one in their field. They coached me and influenced me either directly

or indirectly.

I'd like to thank **Mayooran Senthilmani**, Finance Director, Publisher and Author, for his technical knowledge to make this and my forthcoming publications possible.

I need to mention a few other special people for their precious help and support.

Many thanks to **Patricia Prett**, Project Development Manager and to **Amelia Prett**, Performance Artist, for their valuable editing advice.Many thanks to **Prasanthika Mihirani**, Professional Graphic Designer -SwissCreations, regarding her creativity and her patience to come to the final desirable book cover.

Also, I would like to thank from the depth of my heart both my son **Marios Georgiades Patriotis**, St. Martins Graphic Designer & Ceramics Artist and **Amelia Prett** Performance Artist, for their inspirational design that accompanies the poem "IT WASN'T SO LONG"

I want to leave behind a legacy for two very special men in my life:
My two sons **Photi and Mario Georgiades**. I hope one day each one of them will make their contributions in the world and share their stories.

Thank you for purchasing this book and I hope that by reading this book you will enhance and change your life for the better.

Despina Georgiades Nicolaou

DESPINA G. NICOLAOU

FOREWORD

If you think of each day of your life as a dance, you have to admit that dancing by yourself could be a bit strange after a while, and when looking around at other couples who are dancing together, "for better, for worst" you want that powerful energy called Love, to knock on your door too.

I was interviewing a photographer last week and he was telling me that there is nothing like the day you get married. And I asked him Why? His answer was very sad, but, I guess, true to some extent:" Marital dissolution is contagious. 50% will divorce and re-marry; even if it is good business for me as a photographer. I wish I had more business from the same couple when they celebrate their life union, not when they re-marry. Some people eat honey with a very big spoon, some don't like Honey at all; perhaps, this is why being a divorce lawyer is such good business!"

Most people choose to waltz away their life and understand that it takes two to tango but walk on that aisle without even thinking of what it takes to "live happily ever after".

What do you expect from Marriage?

What influences a couple's risk of divorce?

What are the cultural and political identities that may impact your marriage patterns?

Despina Nicolaou, The Author of The T.R.U.T.H. of Marriage, shares her love story, how she and her husband, George, started their journey together as young adults in love in Greece and how their love grew stronger than ever, after surviving economic loss, recession, depression, uprooting themselves and their family from their country of origins, migrating to London and then to Cyprus, the exhilarating challenges, twists, and turns of faith and how they embrace them and brace each other, at every step of the way, to become the strong love they are at present.

You heard me, become love! On reflection, Love is not about falling in and out of love, or being loved, but being LOVE.

The very fabric of Love, the magic of your love life, is as much Passion as it is Respect and they balance each other, as your vows are renewed each day when you wake up next to the love of your life and feel humbled and grateful for what you hold and respect.

Despina reminds me of the companion of the goddess Nemesis, Aidos, who was the goddess of reverence and respect, the spirit of modesty, who helped mankind from wrong doing.

Before you go on that aisle, before you ring that divorce lawyer, read this book and listen in to Despina's weekly Radio Show "Family Matters" - which could help you find your own T.R.U.T.H.

Marina Nani

Author, Founder, Radio W.O.R.K.S. World

DESPINA G. NICOLAOU

PROLOQUE

Many times in my life I was wondering why I had to face all these difficult situations. Why nobody told me what I should do when facing difficult and challenging times.

I believe to the beauty of marriage not because it joins two people that love each other in a common life but because marriage is the highest happiness in our earth society.

A great percentage of people, men and women, today in the 21st century, believe that marriage is an old fashioned custom and that they can find happiness in lots of other ways.

Through these pages, I will try to explain why marriage is so important and why it is considered to my humble opinion the optimum, the highest happiness.

Through these pages, I want to reach each and every one of you woman separately and walk with you to the path that will guide you to the light.

I know, that by having this book in your hands it means that you already decided to make your efforts for a happy marriage, either you are ready to get married or you are already in a marriage and you are struggling to make it work!

It is not just a simple recipe, I will give you the powerful ingredients, but you have to use them correctly in order to make your sweet called 'HAPPY MARRIAGE' very tasty.

Think about yourself to be in a kitchen, with different ingredients on the table, trying for the first time to cook a sweet. You go up and down, around you it's a kind of mess, and you are sweating by trying not to make a mistake. You know that you have to use one by one all the ingredients correctly to have the desirable result. Above all every member of your family, husband and children can't wait for the moment to try it. They go and come around you, waiting for you to finish it, cook it and serve it. No-one can do this sweet so perfect and so tasty except you, because while you are making this sweet you don't put just the ingredients; you put your love, your passion, all your efforts into making it because you know that it will give so much happiness to them.

What happens at the end? You are so satisfied that your family loved your sweet, that you are sitting aside, watching them, enjoying the results so much that you don't want to try it. You feel full up; for you it is enough that you gave them the joy of a tasty cake. This is your reward!

Let's do the same with your marriage! Based on ten fundamental truths we will try together to follow the recipe and cook together your 'Happy Marriage'!

Take action, you cannot sit back and hope for a Happy Marriage, you have to create the marriage of your dreams.

DESPINA G. NICOLAOU

TRUTH #1 *RESPECT*

"Respect yourself and others will respect you"
Confucius

Have you ever thought about this? Have you realized how important it is to respect yourself? When you learn how to respect yourself then automatically you will know how to show your respect to others as well.

How do you know what you don't know?
Sometimes we can't see the woods for the trees (the old saying)!
Sometimes we miss obvious things to other but we are so close.
We can't see it and "Respect" is one of such vital area.

'Respect' has different meanings for different people. According to the dictionary, it means **a feeling of admiration**. With our busy life, going to work looking after the family, different social obligations, sometimes we don't make time to look at the most important things. Like rusting, eating away the things those were once strong!

We do not show respect to someone by doing what he/she wants and even more we do not demand respect just because we believe that others should respect us. Respect, is something we have to earn.

It is for those that deserve it, not for those who demand it.

Respect, is one of life's greatest treasures! In my opinion it is the cornerstone of any successful marriage. Respect is the first thing you have to give to your spouse, to the one that you love and want to share your life with.

With this treasure in your pocket let's start the journey for a wonderful, happy marriage. Let's take together a deep breath and step by step, allow you to find the path to the light. If you want to make it work, then it will.

So, a respectful person, in this case a respectful wife or a respectful mother is the one that shows respect. She shows her **admiration** to her husband and children with many ways during day and night. Even, if you keep your silence in certain situations you show your respect. You don't always have to say something in order to receive respect (It's like when the teacher enters the classroom and the children go completely silent).

The question is how do we achieve this and why we do not receive respect? The answer is simple, learn how to show the real respect to yourself and instantly you will experience the others respect.

It is very important here to understand that

everything starts from yourself and ends with yourself. With respect, you represent your character, you represent your ideology.

For example, and in this specific case of respect, you have to learn how to show admiration to yourself. You have to WORK for it, every day. You have to try to make yourself and your character better and better.

Think about it! How many times have you wondered how some women are so successful and how they find the way to have everyone and everything next to them, supporting them, loving them, and helping them? How many times have you wondered what is wrong, why this is not happening to you, why everything is just a mess? Although you have started your marital life with the best conditions, everything has changed for the worst.

It's simple. These women are not so successful, loved and respected by accident. They work hard for it, every day, they try to improve themselves. They don't only demand it, they give you something to respect. You have to find the way to admire yourself, to respect yourself; only then your husband and children will respect you. Take a piece of paper and write down some incidents you remember that you didn't receive the respect you expected.

- Try to remember what your reaction was

- What words have you used?
- Was it a constructive discussion or a fight?
- Have you tried to make your husband understand your point of view?
- Were your feelings or the tone of your voice aggressive?

Draw three columns. On the first one write the incident, for example that you and your husband decided to buy a new car. On the second column write what was your position about this decision, what have you said. On the third column write your husbands position, what he said and below how this was ended. Let's make this experiment together, without respect and with respect, presented on the RESPECT AND NON RESPECT GRAPHIC TABLES (Table 1 & 2).

You see how obvious and how easy you receive respect when you show respect. And above all, both of you are happy for the decision; even the buying of a new car was postponed.

There is an old saying 'Do you want to be right or do you want to keep the marriage?'

If you believe that you are right and you are losing the game, just say to your husband that you want to discuss this later, when everyone is calm. Tell him that you want the best solution and that you love him so much that you don't want to fight with him.

This is the same attitude you must have with your children as well. From my personal experience, most of the time, we parents, do not agree with them. The reasons are many, but the most important is fear. We are afraid that something bad may happen to them. But do not forget to show respect to their decisions. Miraculously, this respect will return back to you with all the good results this attitude may bring. You must have in mind that children have their own personality from the moment they are born. It is very important to remember that when you finish with your children and they become adults, the rest of the world has to live with them, so please teach them Respect!

NEVER EVER use bad words or gestures. And like my mum would say:

> **"You catch many more flies with Honey instead of vinegar".**

WITHOUT RESPECT LOVE IS LOST!

Table 1:

INCIDENT	YOUR POSITION	HUSBANDS POSITION
BUY A NEW CAR	WE DON'T HAVE THE MONEY	WE WILL FIND THE MONEY
	I DON'T LIKE THE COLOUR	I LIKE THIS COLOUR
WITH NO RESPECT	I PREFER A FAMILY ONE	I PREFER A SPORT ONE
	LET'S BUY A SMALLER ONE	I WANT A BIG CAR
	ITS BETTER TO KEEP THE OLD ONE	I WANT TO CHANGE IT

The husband bought the car that he wanted and you had the feeling that he didn't show any respect to you

Table 2:

INCIDENT	YOUR POSITION	HUSBAND'S POSITION
BUY A NEW CAR	IT,S A GOOD IDEA BUT HOW DO YOU BELIEVE WE'LL FIND THIS AMOUNT	DON'T WORRY MY LOVE. I THOUGHT ABOUT THIS. LET'S DECIDE AND WE WILL DISCUSS IT.
	DO YOU THINK THAT THIS IS A NICE COLOUR?	WHY, DO YOU HAVE SOMETHING ELSE IN YOUR MIND?
WITH RESPECT	HAVE YOU THOUGHT ABOUT A FAMILY ONE? IN A WHILE WE ARE GOING TO HAVE OUR FIRST BABY	WELL, I DON'T KNOW, REALLY I HAVEN'T THOUGHT ABOUT THIS
	WHY DON'T WE THINK ABOUT A SMALLER ONE FOR THE MOMENT UNTIL WE ARE SURE ITS WHAT WE REALLY WANT?	I LIKE THIS ONE BABY IT IS MY DREAM
	O.K, LETS KEEP THE OLD ONE FOR SOME MORE TIME UNTIL WE MANAGE TO BUY THE ONE THAT YOU LOVE!	O.K BUT NOT FOR LONG

The husband agreed with you for the moment, he showed respect because you were respectful to him.

Personal Notes:

TRUTH #2 *PATIENCE*

"Patience is bitter, but its fruit is sweet"
Aristotle, Greek Philosopher

What really is patience and how far can it go? For most of us, the length of patience is from 5 minutes to a maximum of one day. What does this mean? That we do not have patience at all.

Patience in many cases may take years and rarely a whole life. Patience, according to the dictionary, is the state of endurance under difficult circumstances. Like my grandmother used to say to my mother? "Patience, my daughter, take it slow and it will work itself".

Patience is a very important element of a happy marriage. Marriage has many challenges and you have to exercise yourself in patience. Most of the time, because we do not have patience, we succeed the contrary of the desirable results.

Patience is like your third eye, it is the eye of your soul. It is closed and you have to practice it to open and see things that you cannot see with both your eyes. It will not open the moment you want it to, it does not work like your other eyes that opens or closes whenever you want.

No, this eye opens very very slowly. If you learn to

WAIT, it will allow you to see things clearer, certain situations and people to change. All become easier and better.

W . A. I. T, use your

Wisdom
Ability
Intelligence
Truthfulness

It is also very important, to learn first to have patience with yourself. This will allow you to understand what it means to have patience with all things.

Many potentially good and happy marriages are destroyed because of the lack of patience. When you ask, what happened, why are you divorced? Many women and men answer, "I got tired, I ran out of patience" or "I didn't have the patience to try anymore to continue".

Have you ever thought, why do you see very few happy couples around you? Is it because these few women were lucky and found their other half? Is it because their life was nice and easy? Is it because they don't have financial problems? NO, NO, NO, do not have illusions. The only difference is because these women never gave up, they insisted on trying to make it work, they gave time to all their problems, and they had PATIENCE.

Here I want to make you use your imagination in order to understand that this success, this healthy happy marriage, this result that you see, is not just this.

Imagine a small beautiful green island in the middle of a blue sea, surrounded with blue crystal waters, a shining sun, the birds singing and the habitants of this island very happy. You see them and you want also to live like them, to have their life, you want to be as happy as they are.

You decide to do the same; you go and buy another small island next to theirs. Now you are sure that you will become as happy as they are and you will have the same life as they do.

At the beginning everything is fine. Every day you enjoy your swimming in the blue crystal waters, the beautiful island, the fresh fish, the delicious fruits, you rest enough and everything is perfect.

Suddenly the weather starts to change. Small clouds are concentrated to the sky. You do not give any attention and you smile with your neighbors on the next island because they give too much attention to these tiny, harmless clouds.

A few days later, the clouds return back but this time

bigger and darker. You look at them and you say "It's not a problem, they will go away like the other time, the weather will become better and the sun will shine again above my island". You look to the next island, you see your neighbours who have already started to fix their house, to cut wood for the fireplace, to bring food to the store, to sew heavier clothes and you laugh. "What are they doing? What bad may happen to this beautiful island?"

After a month, big, dark clouds return back and cover all the sky.
You can't see the sun anymore, the birds left, the sea is not calm anymore and big waves hit the shore. The weather is so bad; the wind is so strong that it has destroyed part of the neighbor's roof. Nothing happened to your house. You stay in and you wait until the storm passes. The neighbours work all day and night and with hard work they managed to almost fix the roof but before they complete it, a bigger storm hit them again and the roof collapsed. Yours luckily is safe.

They started again from the beginning, working hard, staying late at night, very sad but with patience fixing their roof and hoping and waiting that things will become better.

In the next storm, the roof was ready and the neighbour's stayed safe underneath it. But this time your roof was hit. Everything collapsed. You have to fix it. You start to do the same, but while fixing it you are complaining by saying "If I knew that storms will hit this island I would never buy it". Anyway, at the end you fixed it.

The winter is long and the storms become a usual phenomenon to your island. For a second time the storm hit your roof. This time you don't do the same as your neighbours. You take your boat and angrily you say "I don't have the patience to build and rebuild this roof all the time. I don't want this kind of life" and you leave.

The next summer you pass with your boat outside of the two islands. You see again your neighbours, happily enjoying the sun, the sea and their beautiful island. Your island is abandoned; your house has no roof.
And then you realize what you did. You say to yourself "How stupid was I, if I had more patience, I would be enjoying my island now!"

Patience is not just waiting; it is the companion of wisdom. You must use your great potential strength that our Creator stored in your mind. With patience, you show your love to others, your husband and your children. With patience everything is solved, becomes better, you can succeed a complete turnaround in bad situations.

Remember that in your marriage a moment of anger

may destroy
everything but a moment of patience may save you of great regret.

God endowed especially women with big reserves of patience. The only thing we have to do is to learn how to use it.

> Patience has many faces.
> Patience with your husband and children has
> the face of love,
> Patience with yourself, in bad situations, has
> the face of hope,
> Patience with God has
> the face of faith.

You may experience struggles, failures, risks, late nights, doubts, changes, disappointments, rejections, sacrifices in your marriage.
Do not give up; remember that every marriage faces this. If you want to make it work, if you want people to say "look at them, how happy that couple is". If you want to get old and have happy children and grandchildren around you, if you want a really healthy family, make it work! Use your ability of patience, learn to be patient and like they say in Greece

> "Αγάλι, αγάλι, γίνεται η αγουρίδα μέλι'
> 'Agali, agali ginete I agourida meli-greekglish"

which means

"Slowly, slowly the sour grape becomes sweet like honey".

Personal Notes:

TRUTH #3 *TRUST*

"I'm not upset that you lied to me, I'm upset that from now on I' can't believe you"
Friedrich Nietzsche

Trust is another fundamental truth. It is the foundational principle that holds your relationship.

According to the dictionary trust is the
"Firm belief in the reliability, truth or ability of someone or something". Also, means "Acceptance of the truth of a statement without evidence or investigation"

Let's remember what we women, do the first time we meet a man that we like. All our senses, our eyes, our ears, our hands, our lips work like x-rays. Is it true? Oh, yes! From our first date we almost have the 90% of the x-ray results. What these results are? Like, "He looks a loyal, integer character, I like him… I think I can **trust** him"
Or
"I don't like him, he looks frivolous, not a serious person, I can't **trust** him".

You see, there is no way a woman who meets a man to characterize him without the word **"trust"**.

Like the doctors use special scientific vocabulary to say or write their findings, we women, always use our x-rays findings of the word trust.

Trust is before love. It is impossible to love a person if you do not trust them. It is like the glue that sticks two pieces together. It is the glue of your marriage.

The question is what do we do, to keep this glue so strong. What do we do to ensure that these two pieces, man & wife will not unglue?

You demand from your husband to be a trustful one. It is not only this. You have to be a trustful one for him as well. You ought to work for this every day in your marital life. From tiny things to bigger ones you have to ensure the trustiness of your spouse. It is not difficult at all. You have only to be true and genuine.

Each and every day of your marital life gives you many opportunities to show him that you are a trustful person.

How?
- The way you take decisions
- The way you act in difficult situations, in dangerous ones
- The way you behave in fun times

At every moment show to your spouse your abilities. He won't trust you with words but with actions.

Please, do not make the mistake that most women do. Do not try to cheat your spouse.
If you succeed in cheating him it doesn't mean that he is fool. It means that he trusted you more than you deserved.

There are no excuses. Even a small lie sometimes can destroy the trust that you have built for years. Like my mother used to say:
"**Trust,** my daughter is like a vase. Once it is broken, though you can fix it, it will never be the same again".

There is another question here. What is your position considering your trustiness to your spouse? Well, here your duty is more difficult. What do I mean?

Let's take the best scenario that you are married for many years, you love each other, you have a happy marriage and also you think that you trust each other. Once you were invited for Christmas Eve from a colleague of your husband. You knew him very well because he had become a very good friend to both of you! Both of you were very happy and excited. You knew that it would be a wonderful Christmas Eve. As soon as you arrived, your friend started to introduce you to all his guests. Among the guests was a very beautiful lady, dressed very sexy. You realized that your husband knew her. She was working for the same company. At the beginning everything was going smoothly. But at the table, you noticed that your husband was very polite with this lady, who by coincidence was sitting opposite him. All your senses made you want to watch her and your husband.

The dinner finished and it was time to dance. He danced with you, and after he went and asked the lady to dance with him. You started to feel insecure, a bit jealous but you still had patience.
To your surprise, you saw him after the end of the dance, to continue dancing with her, the next one as well. Your cheeks became red, you were angry, jealous and you were almost sure that they had been having an affair. Your husband finished his dance and returned back to you full of joy. As soon as he approached you, you said to him that you were not feeling well and you wanted to go home". You said goodnight to all and left. In the car, your husband asked you "What is happening baby? Is it the food that destroyed your appetite?" and you answered "No, it was you, that destroyed my appetite!." And you ruined your beautiful Christmas Eve by arguing.

This is a very bad tactic. Why? Because after having so many years together, you trusted each other and suddenly you question your trustiness to him. I'm not saying to be naïve, but you judged him because of the kindness he showed to a beautiful lady and because of two dances. This is not a serious cause for such behaviour.

If you don't have proof, if you don't know anything, it is no good to judge him. I am not saying to lose your own voice, not at all but first learn how to listen. There are so many explanations for his behaviour, not just the one you thought. This could happen to you! Would you like your husband to ruin your Christmas Eve in a way like this?

Please do not say 'It is not the same" In marriage, everything is the same for both of you, not 50%-50% but 100%-100%. If you really trust someone, less control is needed; therefore there is more freedom in the marriage. This is what we, women, want. Freedom in our marriage. Think about it. If you want freedom you must learn to give freedom. If you want to be trusted you must learn to trust. We trust not only when everything is well. Especially show your real trustiness when clouds are above your family.

"Relationships never die a natural death. They are always murdered by attitude, behavior, ego or ignorance"

NO TRUST=NO RELATIONSHIP

Personal Notes:

TRUTH # 4 *PASSION*

"The measure of a man is what he does with power"
Plato -Greek Philosopher

"All human actions have one or more of these seven causes:
Chance, Nature, Compulsion, Habit, Reason, **Passion** and Desire."
Aristotle-Greek Philosopher

According to the dictionary Passion is "a strong emotion usually related to love or anger". There are people that live for their passion, whatever it is. From the perspective of love they are passionate with their job, their hobby, with politics, philosophy, religion, with their dream, with their spouse, with their children, with their family.

When you are passionate with something whatever it is, there is no reason you will not succeed to your final goal. Just follow your passion and it will lead you to your purpose. You do not need talent to do this.

What about your passion in marriage. In my opinion passion is your marriage juice. It is like the blood in veins. Without this your veins will dry and die. Your marriage will dry out and die.

Every day, every moment you have to show your passion to your spouse and later to your children as well.

You decided to get married because you were in love and your passion for each other drove you to this decision. Both of you dreamt of a wonderful happy marriage. Ok, you get married. End of story. This is what you dreamt? Just to get married? No, this is the start of a wonderful, happy life. The only thing you have to do is to follow your passion.

Do things in your marriage with passion or not at all. Whatever you do, do it with all your heart. 'Follow your passion' not just with words.
It is not just a status; it is not just a "like" in your feelings and finish. Be prepared to work hard and do sacrifices to achieve this happy, successful marriage. Nobody followed one's passion by sitting and waiting!

I want to give you some examples of passion in marriage. (Always have in mind that this book is giving key strategies to women and I'm not referring to men's equal obligations in a marriage).

Let's take together, as an example, that you are a woman who is not passionate with her marriage. What is your attitude as a non passionate married woman?

1) You decided that there isn't a necessity to show your love to your spouse so often. And what is the excuse? "We are not newlyweds, we are not like the first time, we are not so young to show our love every moment"

2) You decided that there isn't a necessity to kiss him every time he is living or coming back home. He knows that "you love him" this is your excuse first to yourself and then to the others.

3) You cook food just to feed him and very often you serve this food for two or three days because you don't have time.

4) You clean the house just because you have to clean it and not because you want a nice and peaceful home with an environment full of good energy.

5) If you have children, you are trying to make them as quiet as you can because you want to rest, watch TV, text and talk on your mobile with your friends or sitting for hours chatting on Facebook.

What are the results for such a kind of marriage? It will die; there is no chance to have the marriage you dreamt. Why? Because you didn't give any attention to it. The passion juice is so few. One day, you will wonder what you have done wrong, but it would be too late. You just didn't follow your passion.

Let's take the example that you are a passionate woman with your marriage. What is your attitude?

1) Every day you show your spouse your love, by calling him for just a second to see if he is well or sending a message of love, just to remind him that you love him and you are looking forward to seeing each other when both of you return back from your jobs. You never forget the date you met, you organise romantic picnics, enjoy your holidays like it was your first time together.

2) Every time your spouse comes in or goes out of the house you kiss him. You feel so nice when you do this. You show to him that you still love him but also this kiss means 'be careful, I'm here waiting for you to return back".

3) Although you return back home tired you love to cook a nice food to enjoy it together. You know exactly what he desires and you try to surprise him as well with new recipes. I would like to say something I like here very much- Greek women from Smyrni named as Smyrnies (they were famous for their delicious cuisine) were saying "Love passes

first from the stomach"

4) You clean the house, you take care of it, you like nice furniture (not necessarily expensive ones), you love paintings and every day you try to have a flower in the vase.

5) If you have children you enjoy when they make noise around you, you cook for all the family and you don't care if you are tired or not. You spend your free time playing with them, reading with them, hearing their problems and trying to help them. If you have some free time, you would then decide to call your friends and sit in front of your laptop.

What are the results for such kind of marriage? It's simple! It will become a successful happy one. When you do things with passion, when you do them with all your heart and when you never ask yourself if it's realistic or not, the success is inevitable.

Oprah Winfrey said 'The biggest adventure you can take is to live the life of your dreams". Think about it. You can, you are able, it is feasible, you deserve it, just be passionate with it.

I also want you to think about a piece of iron eaten by rust. Now think of this iron as your marriage and the rust is your indifference. Day by day, year by year, the iron will be consumed and at the end there will be nothing left.

Now, think about the same piece of iron that you are taking care of. You protect it; you do not leave it exposed in the air, the rain, the dust and humidity. You always work hard to keep it in the right conditions. Day by day, year by year your piece of iron will stay the same, strong and shiny. This is the way you have to think about marriage.

When you have passion you do not wait for the storm, you work hard, you dream, you make sacrifices and at the end you learn

HOW TO DANCE IN THE RAIN!

Personal Notes:

TRUTH # 5 *LOVE*

"Why you wrote to her 'I can't live without you'
Why you wrote to him 'I can't live without you'
and you went East and she went West and both of you lived separate".
Odysseas Elytis Greek poet

Concerning the above I could say that "You really shouldn't say 'I love you' unless you mean it. But if you mean it, you should say it a lot. Remember Love never fails.

Love according to the dictionary means a strong feeling of affection and sexual attraction for someone.

As a married woman, or a woman that is about to get married it means that you are in love with a man and decided to share your lives together; you decided to stay by his side for the rest of your life; you gave your heart to him because he was the only one that made you feel you were the special one; you allowed for his soul to touch your soul, you trusted him and let yourself lean on his shoulders. It means that your eyes and your soul are being reflected in his eyes and these eyes become your mirror.

All these thoughts and much more are almost the same causes for a woman to decide that she is ready to get married. But marriage is not an easy decision.

My grandmother used to say to my mother 'Marriage is like a bottle full of sour juice and on top is the honey. At the beginning the taste is sweet but slowly, slowly it becomes sour'

I could say that a big percentage of this statement is true. Why? Because marriage needs sacrifices, hard work, risk, struggles, disappointments, doubts, changes, persistence. For love it is the same. It needs lots of actions on behalf of your side, the woman's side, in order to keep love's presence in your marriage.

From my personal experience I would like to give you some tips about love and some examples as well. Before I do this, I want you to write on the hard disc of your mind and never delete this **'There is no recipe for love'.** There are all kinds of love in this world but never the same love twice. This means that my criteria's of love are different to yours. Also, I'd like to make it clear to you that if you want to give love you must love yourself first. Only then will you be able to give love.

Let's make a graph to show you what love is. Let's draw my grandmother's bottle of marriage but this time we'll name it the bottle of love and more precisely the perfume of love.

THE T.R.U.T.H OF MARRIAGE

You go to a beauty shop and you see this beautiful perfume called "LOVE" and you want it. You smell it, its aroma is intoxicating and you suddenly have the impulse to have it.

If I was to tell you that I have the recipe of this perfume in order for you to have it for a lifetime, would you like me to tell you what it is? I almost hear your YESes;

Well here I give you the Love recipe.

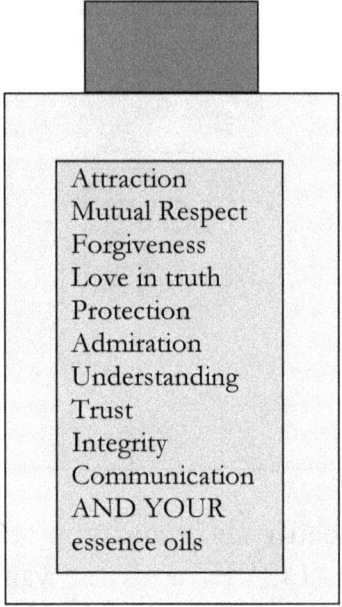

Remember there is no same Love Recipe for everyone. You have to add your essence oils to this recipe.

I know what you are thinking, 'it is not easy to find all these ingredients. Can I do this perfume with fewer ingredients, with only the ones that I already have?

The answer is NO, because every woman can. Do not forget that Mother Nature forethought and endowed women with huge reserves of love. Only a woman can give so much love around her, because she is the chosen one to give birth to new lives. Do not forget that every woman is capable, love yourself believe in yourself and do not have doubts that you will make this recipe a successful one.

Let love guide your life. Do not be anxious, loving your spouse forever is one of your best decisions in your life. Maybe forever seems like a long time and that it is difficult to achieve but believe me time runs so fast, you won't realize when you were young and suddenly you are in the middle age.

Do not give up when you face difficulties, struggles, doubts because giving up is what makes a situation permanent.

I want to tell you the love story of a friend of mine. Unfortunately it ended with a divorce because few ingredients (our recipe's ingredients) were used in this relationship.

He was studying in London and she just finished at the Medical School University in Athens. It was August and all the students at the Medical School decided to organize a beach party at Vouliagmeni beach. They wanted to celebrate their graduation.

The full moon is the biggest in August. The sea was so calm like oil, the reflection of the moon on the sea sparkling like gold fallen from heaven, the fires, the songs, the guitars and the smell of the fish that the students were cooking on the charcoals plus the cold beers made that night unique.

At that night my friend met her husband. He was

invited by another friend of hers. Their love was love at first sight. It was full of passion and both of them were great personalities, good characters, very clever and both of them from good families.

He was going and coming from London very often and sometimes he was keeping it a secret from his parents that he was in Athens because he wanted to have all his time just for her.

After he finished his studies, he returned back and as soon as he found a job they decided to get married. Their marriage was a dreamy one.

Everything at the beginning was perfect, like my grandmothers bottle, but slowly, slowly the clouds started to gather above their marriage. Why? What was the problem? They had everything for having a good marriage. They started with good jobs, with no financial problems; they bought a new apartment, new furniture and a new car. They had everything plus the fact that both of them were very good people.

Their problem was that two ingredients were missing from their love recipe. From her side, forgiveness and from his side understanding. She wasn't in a position to forgive some things in her marriage from tiny ones to more serious. Every time they had a fight she was bringing up mistakes from the past in their discussions.

From his side, every time they were arguing he didn't want to give any space for understanding. He always wanted to win an argument.

That situation lasted for years, because both of them used their essences oils to keep their marriage. Finally they got divorced in their fifties when they had three grown children. They didn't realize that their love bottle didn't have all the necessary ingredients. Time was passing and the other ingredients of their love bottle, like trust, admiration, and communication started to evaporate.

At the end there was nothing left and divorce was inevitable.
So,

1. Never be angry with your spouse when he is angry with you.

2. Never yell at each other.

3. Do not always want to win an argument. If you are wise let him win or at least let him believe that he has won.

4. Do not criticize your spouse without being polite.

5. Never bring up mistakes from the past in your discussions.

6. Never ever accuse your husband to friends & relatives. Everything that happens to your house must stay in your house (family). There is an ancient saying «ΤΑ ΕΝ ΟΙΚΩ ΜΗ ΕΝ ΔΗΜΩ» which means that everything that happens in your home, to your family, keep it away from the public.

7. Never go to sleep with an argument unsettled.

8. Try everyday to show your love to your spouse. It is not necessary to do big things, besides the small ones are more important. Show your love to him with a kiss, with tasty food, with candles, flowers, take care of yourself, it is very important to be always beautiful, dressed well and wear fine lingerie. Welcome him, surprise him, and tell him that you love him. Become important to him. Treat him like his is not an ordinary man, that he is a special one.

9. When you are wrong admit it. Do not let ego to grow in between you.

And as Socrates the Greek philosopher would say "I cannot teach anybody anything! I can only make them think".

THINK, TAKE ACTION, LOVE

IT WASN'T SO LONG

It wasn't so long when you and me
young and happy
we were enjoying our love
to this beautiful golden sandy beach.

It wasn't so long when the bright stars
the full moon, the whisper of the sea
and this sandy beach
were celebrating with us, because
"JUST MARRIED"

It wasn't so long when the sun,
the sky blue sea
and the same golden sandy beach
opened their arms to welcome our children.

Now, we are sitting alone to
our golden sandy beach paradise
and we recall all these marital beautiful memories
and we say to each other
"It wasn't so long................."

But I know no matter how many years
will pass
together to the same path of life
we will hold each other and we will always say
"It wasn't so long............."

The design was inspired by Marios Georgiades Patriotis, St.Martins Graphic Designer &Ceramics Artist and Amelia Prett Performance Artist.

Personal Notes:

TRUTH #6 *LOYALTY*

"The strength of a family, like the strength of an army, is in its loyalty to each other"
Mario Puzo American Author

"Love is absolute loyalty. People fade, looks fade, but loyalty never fades"
Sylvester Stalone actor

According to the dictionary loyalty means "A strong feeling of support or allegiance" like "she is known for her loyalty to her family" or "He was honored for his extreme loyalty to the Crown".

Loyalty, like the other truths we examined so far, is very important to a relationship and in this case in marriage. When it comes to relationships remaining loyal is not an option but a priority.

To be loyal to your spouse and later on to your children it will help you to create a strong relationship with the family.

Nowadays, unfortunately loyalty as like other life values has become a tattoo or graffiti on a wall; the meaning of 'slavery' was given to loyalty because it is an easy way for modern societies to avoid obligations and excuse the wrong attitude in a relationship.

Both of you decided through marriage to follow the river of life in good and bad times. Your join makes you strong and even stronger when there is loyalty between both of you.

Loyalty is rare and always returned back when you give it with all your heart. When you stand by your spouse in bad times, being loyal not only in good times but also when things really suck, allows you to deserve to be there when good times come. This is what makes your relationship perfect.

Of course not only in bad times is your loyalty tested but your spouses' as well. His loyalty is tested even more so when the good times come and he has everything he ever dreamed.
Here I want to make clear that we are not loyal to someone according to our need of him. What do I mean? I mean that lots of women (I'm referring to women because we study the Truth of marriage from women's side) decide to get married because the status of the specific marriage will cover certain personal needs they have.

For example, they get married because of money, of power, of fame. They are loyal to them until their needs change. If opportunity controls your loyalty it means that you will never manage to make a real family.

The real loyalty is to stay real and supportive with all

your being to your man in bad times as well, when your man has nothing to give you. Remember loyalty is not pretending to have beliefs, virtues, feelings; this is hypocrisy. Loyalty is one ring of the chain that makes your family, a FAMILY.

Loyalty may involve sacrifices. Nobody said the contrary. The paths to the light are always difficult but remember the difficult paths guide you to beautiful places.

Let's give an example of loyalty and one of non-loyalty.

You are a young woman, at the last year of your University degree and in your summer vacation in a beautiful island you meet the man of your life. You spend all your time by the beach, you enjoy every minute together, fall in love with each other and by the end of your vacation you decide that you have a lot in common and would like to get married.

You go back to your country and you announce to your parents your decision. Your parents respect your decision but they want you to continue your studies in University and take your degree and marry once it is completed.

So, you go back to your partner and tell him that you are going to marry him but you have to continue your studies for another year in order to take your degree.

You get married and then leave for University. During this year although you were far away from your husband you stayed loyal to him. Every day you had communication with him, telling him about your daily program, your agonies, and how much you missed him and were looking forward to finishing and returning back to him.

All this time you stayed real, faithful and loyal; you looked after him although you were far away and you wanted to finish University and return back. You realized that when you get married, your loyalty to your spouse and to the family that you decided to create together comes first.

Now, let's give the same example with non-loyalty.

Again, you meet a young man during your summer vacation and by the end of the summer you decide to get married. Your parents agree with this decision but they want you after your marriage to continue your studies in the University. You need only one year to finish it and take your degree.

You get married and then you leave for your University. During this year you continued your student life like you were free. You had contacts with your husband but most of the times you didn't have time for him because your programme was very heavy. Actually you never had an effective communication with him.

You were pretending that you had feelings for him and that you were looking forward to finishing and returning back to him. Before the end of the year you told him that all graduates decided to go for a trip to Paris to celebrate and then return to their homes.

You didn't ask his opinion, during this year you were not loyal to your marriage but to your personal needs. You didn't look after your spouse or your relationship you only looked after your life.
The meaning of loyalty was misunderstood.

It is very important to say that 'relationships are always murdered by attitude, behavior, ego or ignorance'.

Marriage is the joining of the two to one. It is your breath in his breath! And loyalty is what we seek and it makes all the difference in a marriage.

BE LOYAL TO YOUR MARRIAGE; BE LOYAL TO YOUR FUTURE.

Personal Notes:

TRUTH #7 *HONESTY*

"Honesty is the first chapter of Wisdom"
Buddha

According to the dictionary honesty means the quality or fact of being honest; uprightness and fairness.

In a relationship if there is no honesty and trust there is no point of its existence. "Tell a lie once and all your previous truths will become questionable"

Marriage is not just a ceremony and then it's all finished. Through marriage you and your partner join your lives under the roof of love. Your souls and bodies become one and together you will walk the path of life.

Together you will face the good and the bad but each one must separately support and give strength to each other. There is no point of loving if honesty does not exist in your relationship.

The question is "why you chose to live with this man for the rest of your life?" Give this answer to yourself but be honest and true. If you can't afford to be honest stay single.

Honesty is the cornerstone of the success of your

marriage; one of the best keys to making a good relationship. Be honest with the people who love you. Sometimes it is hard to tell the truth but no matter how hard it is you must not avoid it.

Why? Because, if you tell a lie and sometimes a small lie, then you try to cover it with another lie. It takes so much energy, the errors multiply and you constantly try to cover the one lie with another.

The truth may hurt for a while, but remember a lie hurts forever. Do not behave to others, with the way you don't like others to behave towards you!

In a relationship don't only take care of your external charismas, like to be beautiful and perfect, but also your internal ones. Be truthful and sincere to your spouse, be truthful to yourself and become the person that others can trust.

"No matter how plain a woman maybe, if truth and honesty are written across her face, she will be beautiful"
Eleanor Roosevelt First Lady of USA (1933-1945)

With honesty in your marriage you walk securely, it gives you a sense of freedom and liberation. You do not need to cover the one lie with another and also you don't need to remember what you said.

Remember this: ***A true relationship is when you***

can tell anything and everything to each other. There is no space for secrets and lies.

Let's take two simple examples of honesty and dishonesty and examine the results of being honest or dishonest to your partner.

You are recently married and everything looks so wonderful. You love your husband, you are both happy. Both of you work and already started to make plans for a baby. One day you returned back earlier and while you were in the kitchen, trying to cook his favorite dish, your mobile rings. You were sure that this call was from your husband who every day calls to say that he is on the way home. Unfortunately this call was from an old affair you had before you met your husband. He heard that you had got married and he called you to tell you how stupid he was to let you go from his life and that he still loves you and would like to meet you just for a coffee and a last goodbye.

This call made you so upset, all your good mood disappeared. You knew that this man wasn't the proper one for you and that you do not have any feelings for him. You didn't like that he suddenly appeared in your life and you wanted him not to be around.

Your husband came home, and immediately he realized that something wrong was happening to

you. He asked you if you are well.
Although you never mentioned to your husband this old relationship and in fact you had doubts about his reaction, you decided to be honest and tell the truth.

You said everything to him and both of you decided to face together this guy. You felt such a relief and you were so happy that your husband appreciated your honesty.

Let's take the same example with dishonesty.

You had the same call from your old affair, telling you that he still loves you and wants to meet you. When your husband returned home, although he asked if everything was well, you decided to avoid to tell him the truth.

The reason wasn't because you decided to cheat on him or because you still had feelings about this guy, but because you were afraid to tell your husband the truth. You hadn't mentioned this previous relationship to him and you weren't sure how he would react so you chose to keep it a secret.

The result was that this guy started calling you every day trying to convince you to meet him just once. You started getting upset and nervous and your husband observed that you were thoughtful and absent minded.

In his questions you kept saying lies because it was too late to tell him the truth. Your excuses were like 'I have a headache' or 'my friend is sick and I'm worried about her' and a bunch of lies just because you made the mistake not to tell the truth.

You decided to go and meet this guy and tell him to leave you alone, that you are a married woman that you love your husband and you do not have any more feelings for him.

Unfortunately in this appointment it was not just you and him there. Your husband followed you because he didn't believe you and he was sure that something was wrong.

You felt so embarrassed and although you tried to convince him that nothing was happening between you and this guy, although you promised to him that this will never happen again and from now on you will never lie to him, his reply was "I'm sorry you are not forgiven".

In the first case, the wise decision to be honest with her husband, not only protect herself and her family but also **her honesty was appreciated.**

In the second case, she decided not to be honest with her husband, not to tell him the truth because she was afraid of his reaction. His doubts ruined their relationship.

Honesty is difficult; the truth may hurt but never ever choose the path of dishonesty in your marriage. It will lead you to the rocks.

Tell the truth no matter how hard it is and keep others out of the middle of your relationship.

If something is not right do not do it! If it is not true do not say it!

"NO LEGACY IS SO REACH AS HONESTY"
Shakespeare

Personal Notes:

TRUTH #8 *ATTITUDE*

"A positive attitude can really make dreams come true; it did it for me"
David Bailey English Fashion & Portrait Photographer

Attitude according to the dictionary is 'a position of the body indicating a particular mental state: 'The boy was standing in an attitude of despair' **and** a settled way of thinking or feeling about something like 'Being competitive is an attitude of mind'.

Depending on your attitude, positive or negative, you create beauty and happiness in your life and in this case in your marriage. It is very important to be aware of what you do mentally and physically. It is very important to control your behaviour, your actions and your words.

You are the only person responsible for your attitude in your marriage. There are no excuses. Your attitude is the main cause of the good results in your marriage. It is like when you make a cake. You want a cake but you are bored, you don't want to dedicate some time for this, you don't have time, it is not necessary to follow exactly the recipe's instructions; what is the result? Your cake is no good and above all even the little time you spent on it was wasted as well.

The same thing is in life. When your attitude is negative, you do not allow yourself to see things or understand situations. Remember with good attitude you do good things. Your attitude is your responsibility.

A bad day in your marriage it depends on your attitude. There is no 'I can't'. You can transform a bad day to a good day by changing your attitude.

How many times can you remember yourself and your spouse, having a fight for insignificant reasons? How many times you can remember that when your attitude was positive the end of that fight was good. On the contrary, the fight became serious, because of your selfish attitude. You didn't want to listen, you had all the rights, you always knew what to do, you remembered all the bad previous situations and the list of negative feelings has no end.

Your attitude defines you and your marriage's future. A bad attitude can block love, blessings and destiny from finding you. So, don't be the reason of not having a successful marriage. Do not allow your attitude to stand between you and your spouse.

Anything you do in the present affects your future, your family's future and your children's future. If you see things are not going well, **change your attitude.** The cause of your miserable marital life, most of the time is from your own attitude. From all of the negative attitudes you can imagine in a marriage, selfishness with no gratitude creates a pessimistic attitude.

We women have the key of a successful marriage.

Imagine yourself standing in front of two houses. You are just married and your parents gave you a key. They told you to go to a specific address and there you will find their present. You and your husband are very excited going to that address. In front of you there are two houses. One is a beautiful big one, with lots of windows allowing the light to come in and an imposing door. It has a big garden, planted with beautiful flowers and trees; in the middle there is a swimming pool, surrounded with chairs to relax in.

The other one next to it is a small nice house with two windows on the front side and one usual door. The house has a small garden also planted with beautiful flowers and two trees on the side. In the middle there is a table with chairs to relax in and an umbrella.

You don't know which house you have the key for but you wish the key belongs to the big house. You try it and you realize that the key is not for this house but for the smaller one next door.

There are two scenarios of your reaction. The first

one is that you start complaining by saying 'I've never thought that I was so lucky to have a house like this one' or 'I've lost my mood, I don't really want to see the other one, I don't like it so there is no meaning to try if the key works for the other door or not'.

The second scenario is to try the key in to the big imposing door again. You realize that the key is not for this house but for the next one. You turn to your husband and you say to him "How stupid I am, my parents would never afford to buy us such a big house. It must be the next one. I'm sure the key is for this small beautiful house. I am so excited, what a generous present. I already love this house. Look how beautiful the garden is with all these flowers, and these trees are so big! It is not like the next one, but it will become our love nest won't it? We are going to fix it and make it just how we want it".

You see the negative and the positive attitude.

With the negative attitude her feelings changed. She felt sad, unlucky, like she didn't deserve to have a future in a house like this. If she continues to have this attitude her life will become torture, unhappy and miserable because she will always feel the lack of things that she doesn't have. If she manages to have a house like the bigger one, her attitude will not allow her to enjoy that moment because of the need to have an ever bigger one, a nicer one in a better neighbourhood. Above all her attitude affects the people around her. Imagine her husband's feelings next to her when he sees her reaction.

On the contrary, the reaction that is a positive attitude, created good energy. Her happiness in having the key in her hands became bigger when she saw the house. She started making dreams with her husband and everything was perfect. She didn't stop at the fact that the other house was not for them. She saw the glass half full instead of half empty.

An attitude of gratitude, a positive attitude, helps you to recognize life's "presents". In this way you attract more in life by leaving behind you what is not useful for you to create space for new possibilities in your life.

Improve your attitude by positive thinking, positive affirmation and positive self-talk.

In order for your marriage and your family to be healthy and happy you need to have an attitude of serious, caring involvement in the concerns of others.

If you can't change situations change your attitude. Transform by the renewing of your mind. Attitude is a huge factor in improving yourself. The only disability in life is attitude. And remember

"HAPPINESS IS WHEN, WHAT YOU THINK, WHAT YOU SAY AND WHAT YOU DO ARE IN HARMONY"
Mahatma Gandhi

Personal Notes:

TRUTH # 9 *COMMUNICATION*

"If we have no piece, it is because we have forgotten that we belong to each other"
Mother Teresa

"We have two ears and one mouth, so we can listen twice as much as we speak"
Epictetus Greek Stoic Philosopher

According to the dictionary communication means: "The imparting or exchanging of information by speaking, writing or
using some other medium 'television is an effective means of
communication" also the successful conveying or sharing of ideas and feelings. "There was a lack of communication between Pamela and her parents".

Communication between the couple is the main ingredient for a successful marriage. Communication is the water that is watering your plant 'marriage'. It helps your relationship to blossom and grow.

If there is no communication there is no marriage. Most of the times there is the illusion that there is communication in your marriage. The fact is that the meaning of communication, especially nowadays in our advanced technological world, was misunderstood.

Communication in marriage means talking to each other person to person, and not just

1) Leaving messages on the fridge,
2) Sending SMS with few words and lots of signs like hearts, smiles, ASAP, SOS, etc
3) Quick calls from your mobile giving instructions and that's it.

If you want to be in a successful marriage you have to dedicate time for it. This will not be possible if by the time he comes home you have to leave or the contrary. A big percentage of couples meet each other during weekends and even their sexual life it is programmed. They run like crazy and if you ask them how they allowed their lives to become so busy the only answer they give is
"I don't have time. I have so many things to do; I can't leave behind so many important matters".

They do not realize that they leave behind THE most important.
FAMILY MATTERS.

Communication is to find time every day for both of you, to sit and speak with each other, to tell each other how your day has been seen, to express your feelings, your worries, your ideas, by looking him in his eyes and at the same time touching him, kissing him, telling him that you missed him, and that you are very happy that you are together at the end of the day.

This tactic will help you to improve your relationship, to develop it to higher level and when you have children you will continue your communication with them in the same way as well. This tactic will become a part of your life, it will become a great custom.

When you communicate with your spouse, you have to be very careful how you do this. You have to communicate without arguing or fighting.

Learn how to listen and understand and not how to listen and reply.

It is very important in your communication with your spouse not to let unwholesome talk come out of your mouth. It will not help you at all. On the contrary if you insist to use this way of communication at the end you will succeed by not having any communication which is the worst scenario or a poor communication which is the best scenario.

If you allow to yourself to believe that there is good communication between you and your husband by just making assumptions, this is a big mistake. By communicating with him makes you are 100% sure that everything is o.k.
For example how many times have you heard from

your surroundings that "Mary & John, this wonderful couple, got a divorce". Everybody is wondering why and if you ask John, his reply will be "Yes, Mary is a great woman but since more than a year we didn't have any communication at all and every time we were trying to communicate it ended in big fight" or "I was sure that everything was okay and I was shocked when he told me that he wants a divorce. He told me that there is no communication between us and this is not what he wanted from our marriage".

Never, ever forget that you belong to each other; you are not just two persons. You are like **Aristotle** said "Your love is composed of a single soul inhabiting two bodies" This is the meaning of marriage. A real relationship has fights, has tears, has unnecessary arguments, has jealousy but also has trust, has faith, has tenderness, has kisses and smiles, has patience, has **communication** and above all it has love.

A lot of your problems will disappear if you talk to each other. Don't raise your voice, improve your arguments, tell him that you need to talk to him; don't be afraid to express your feelings to your man. Do not let your ego come between you and say only what is helpful.

I know we live in the century of speed and everything passes in front of us like lightning. But do not allow to yourself to become one more fool that is holding an expensive mobile phone and despite the fact you are sat next to each other, you and your partner prefer to exchange messages through facebook and analyze the silly messages. You want a real relationship not a facebook one.

Communicate with your spouse. By communication you will find your similarities and only then you will respect your differences. Only then you will become two people that want to face life together in its storm.

I would suggest improving your communication with the help of humor. Humor plays an important role in your relationship. It also smoothes tension.

For example add some salt to your relationship while you communicate "I think you are suffering from lack of Vitamin ME" Or "Can I borrow a kiss? I promise I'll give it back".

A true relationship is when you can tell each other anything and everything. I'd like to close this chapter with a **Sufi Saying**

> **Before you speak, let your words pass through three gates:**
> **At the first gate ask yourself**
> **"Is it true?"**
> **At the second gate ask yourself**

DESPINA G. NICOLAOU

"Is it necessary?"
At the third gate ask yourself
"Is it kind?"

Personal Notes:

TRUTH #10 *FRIENDSHIP*

"A faithful friend is a medicine of life"
Bible

"Lots of people want to ride with you in the limo, but what you want is someone who will take the bus with you when the limo breaks down"
Oprah Winfrey

According to the dictionary Friendship means:

1) The state of being a friend; association as friends; to value a person's friendship
2) A friendly relation or intimacy
3) Friendly feeling of disposition

I want to examine with you the meaning of friendship in marriage from two different angles.

1) The friendship between the couple (you and your spouse)
2) The friendship between the couple and other couples (friendly couples of yours)

It is very important to establish with your spouse the institution of friendship in your marriage.

To have your husband not only a lover, a partner but a friend as well, it means that your marriage reached the optimum level. It means that you have applied all of the previous nine truths in your marital life successfully.

Without friendship marriage lacks something. When you are not able to see your husband as a friend it means that something wrong is happening in your marriage.

When couples spend their time together they are more likely to have a happy marriage or relationship. Talk to your husband like you do with your friend, do not be afraid to discuss with him like you do with your best friend, express to him your feelings, your worries, ask him to tell you his opinion, don't be afraid to cry on his shoulders, laugh with him for stupid things, say jokes. If you do this, your marriage will become more fulfilling and exciting.

In the next page there is a graphic.

According to the graphic when there is a friendship between the couple there is perfect match. But when between friendships exists the feeling of love then things become complicated. And when there is sex in friendship things become really messy.

Also very important in your marriage is the friendship between you and other married couples. From various studies a healthy friendship within couple benefits your relationship. To be friends with other couples makes your marital life more fulfilling and exciting providing more understanding and more attraction between you and your spouse.

The reasons are several. When you are next to other couples you observe different behaviours, you understand more about the way that men are behaving and how they negotiate their differences with other women.

Also, your life is more exciting. You know that every weekend you are going to meet if not all of them, some of them or at least one of them. You know that they will be, as friends, next to you in bad and good times.

During Christmas, Easter, or other festive days you will celebrate together, when your children are born will be next to you sharing your happiness. They will share with you all your best moments. When you buy a house, a new car, find a new job, when you establish your business. They should also be next to you in times with health problems, accidents, and financial problems.

What you need are healthy couple friendships, or just healthy friendships. You do not want a lot of friends, you just want FRIENDS.

Get rid of negative people in your marital life. They are able to destroy your happiness. Be very careful with people around your family.

Unfortunately not all people are as good as we think. Behind their smile the jealousy is hidden and they will be very happy to see your life ruined. Learn how to protect yourself, your spouse and your children.

GET RID OF NEGATIVE PEOPLE IN YOUR LIFE!
YOU DO NOT NEED THIS KIND OF DRAMA!

THE T.R.U.T.H OF MARRIAGE

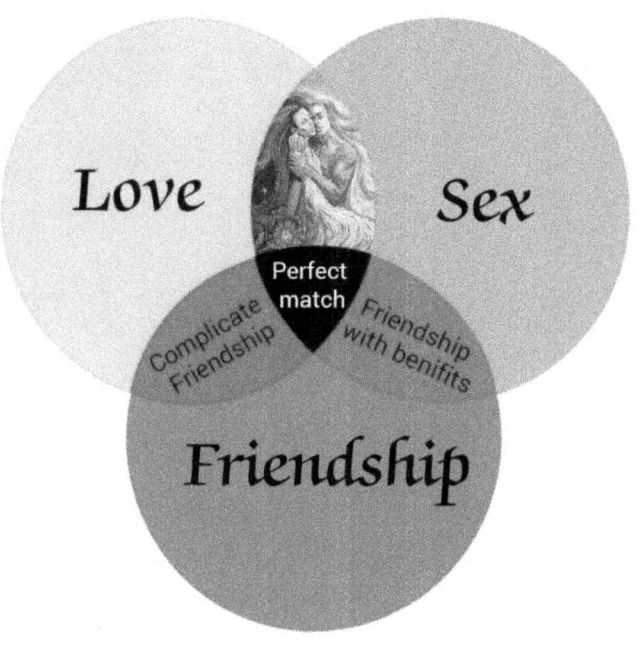

Personal Notes:

EPILOGUE

"Philotimo to the Greek is like breathing. A Greek is not a Greek without it. He might as well not be alive" THALIS *Greek Philosopher*

Philotimo (filotimo) is a word that you do not find in any other vocabulary of any other language, but only in the Greek one. It is a pure and unique Greek word and it consists of two words philo=friend + timi= honor. Which means love of honor. To do what's right and what's honorable.

For Greeks philotimo is a golden rule. It is a great word. It is a complex term. Philotimo is compassion, generosity, duty, honour, decency, dignity, respect, honesty, truthfulness, sincerity, hospitality, love, affection.

From the day we are born until our death this word is a motivating power. It is a motivating power for us but for our children as well.

I remember when I was doing something wrong for example, making too much noise and not caring about disturbing others, and my mother would ask me « Δεν έχεις φιλότιμο? », "Don't you have a philotimo?". Philotimo is a word that I've heard from my parents, my grandparents, my teachers, our priest, from society.

Philotimo is a treasure; it is a word with deep meaning. Every time you deviate from honorable and decent way of living, people will ask you "Don't you have a philotimo?". Philotimo is a word that represents not only you but your family as well.

When you go out to the world you have the responsibility to honour the name of your mother, your father, your husband, your family and your entire community.

While I was writing about these ten fundamental truths this word was always coming into my mind. So, I decided to write a few words about this truly special unique word, packed with positive values.
Keep this word in your mind, use it in your life, and use it when you want to teach values to your children!

ABOUT THE AUTHOR

Despina G. Nicolaou born in Cyprus. At the age of 19 she went to Greece for further education. She studied the French language and took her diploma from the Institute Francaise d'Athenes.

At the same time she improved her secretarial skills that she got from her studies in C.D.A Cyprus, by attending stenography lessons in Athens. She took her diploma from YMCA Athens.
She also attended some business lessons at Deree College Athens.
She got married and she has two sons and a wonderful marriage.

When she was 35 years old she decided to make her own lingerie business. She was the founder of an import & wholesale company and she was representing big brand names in lingerie business from U.S.A and U.K.. She became a successful business woman and her company was among the lingerie leaders in Greece.

Unfortunately the Greek crisis didn't allow further growth of her business, on the contrary year by year her clientele was getting smaller and smaller and her business stopped being profitable. So she and her husband who joined the company later, decided to close their business and see what they could do. At the same time a lot of very bad incidents were happening to their family. It was like the heaven opened and it was raining bad fortune, failures, doubts, changes, disappointments, rejections.

They started from zero and they returned to zero, but together they faced all these surprises good or bad that life reserves for everyone.
When you ask the author about all these she says

"The only thing I can say from all these experiences until now is that we were able to face all these obstacles because our marital life was based in ten fundamental truths. This experience I want to share as a woman with all married women but also with women who are planning to get married. Through this book my aim and my dream is to become helpful and support the cause of a successful healthy marriage".

"WE CANNOT LEARN WITHOUT PAIN"
Aristotle Greek Philosopher

TESTIMONIALS

Despina Georgiades Nicolaou is the author of this wonderful book, (THE T.R.U.T.H OF MARRIAGE). Married to her lifelong partner and husband, George. They have two very talented sons, both respectively pursuing their own career.

One of the most important subjects in life, namely, 'How to have a successful Marriage' is not on any school curriculum. Therefore, it is left to chance that when two people are married, magically, it will be Happy Ever After!

Clearly, we all know this is not the case. No marriage is perfect or plain sailing. The strength of any marriage often only shows itself when faced testing and challenging times.

Both Despina and George have their shares of this, losing their successful business due to the Global financial crisis through no fault of their own and other challenges. Their marriage remains strong and happy despite what life has thrown at them.

By learning her simple, powerful and stimulating tips, she will empower you the Reader with ideas to enrich your married life and for those who are contemplating Marriage.

In this book:

- You will discover new beautiful prospects in marriage

- .You will be able to change your attitude

- You will develop your inner self

- You will communicate the growth of confidence in your children as you practice the skills and tips in this book.

- You will learn how to develop plans and strategies to enrich your marriage.

This book will give you new insight and as important perhaps for your children to see the Role Model that is the best for them-namely, You and Your Spouse.

You will find this book stimulating and informative as I did, while I was reading this book.

Philip Chan
Amazon Best Selling Author
www.jetsetlearning.com

I have known Despina Georgiades Nicolaou for many years.

She is a fair person, a restless soul, a fighter woman always surrounded by people who want her advice for problems which occupy them. And she always treats them with calm, seriousness, impartial, with joy and sincerity.

I felt this book was a natural consequence. Her gained experience certainly made her wise and I'm sure that she is capable to help a lot of women that caged in wrong paths.

Mary Constandourou
Greek Novel Author

Personal Notes:

Personal Notes:

Personal Notes:

Personal Notes: